W0246438

100 Questions & Answers About Social Security

by The Experts at AARP

AARP®

for dummies®
A Wiley Brand

100 Questions & Answers About Social Security For Dummies®

Contents at a Glance

Table of Contents

Introduction

Social Security provides retirement benefits for nearly every American. In fact, around 97 percent of older adults receive Social Security benefits, according to the Social Security Administration. But Social Security isn't just about retirement — it also provides survivor benefits and disability benefits. This book answers common questions about Social Security — what it is, who's eligible for it, how to apply for it, and more.

About This Book

This book is a reference, which means you don't need to read the chapters in order from beginning to end and you don't have to remember anything — there isn't a test at the end of it.

Within this book, you may note that some web addresses break across two lines of text. If you're reading this book in print and want to visit one of these web pages, simply key in the web address exactly as it's noted in the text, pretending as though the line break doesn't exist. If you're reading this as an e-book, you've got it easy — just click the web address to be taken directly to the web page.

Foolish Assumptions

In writing this book, we made just a couple of assumptions about you, the reader:

>> You're on Social Security, you're eligible for Social Security, or you will be eligible for Social Security soon.

>> You have questions, and you want answers.

If those basic assumptions apply to you, you've come to the right place.

Icon Used in This Book

TIP

When you see the Tip icon, you'll find information that will make your life a little easier, at least when it comes to Social Security.

Where to Go from Here

If you aren't sure where to begin, head to the Table of Contents and skim through the questions until you find one that catches your eye. Or, if you have a specific topic in mind, search for it in the Index. Want to know absolutely everything? Turn the page and start in with Part 1.

1

Getting Started with Social Security

IN THIS PART . . .

This part explains what Social Security is and who it's for. It helps you determine whether you're eligible for Social Security. And it explains how to apply for Social Security. If you're new to Social Security, this part is for you.

Chapter **1**

Understanding Social Security

Social Security is a critical benefit to Americans of all ages, especially retirees, the vast majority of whom receive Social Security retirement benefits. This chapter explains the basics — what Social Security is, where the money comes from, whether it will run out someday, and more.

What Is Social Security?

Social Security is a federal social insurance program in the United States administered by the Social Security Administration (SSA). It provides financial support for retirees, surviving spouses, children of deceased workers, and people with disabilities.

What Is the Social Security Number?

The Social Security number (SSN) is a nine-digit number used to identify people in the United States. It was created in 1936 as part of the implementation of the Social Security Act of 1935. It's written like this: AAA-GG-SSSS. Originally, the first three numbers (AAA) showed where you lived when you got the number, the middle two (GG) were used to sort records, and the last four (SSSS) were just a sequence. As of 2011, the government assigns these numbers randomly to make them more secure. Over time, the SSN has become a key way to identify people for things like jobs, taxes, and government benefits.

What Are the Social Security Trust Funds?

The Social Security trust funds are two financial accounts managed by the U.S. Department of the Treasury:

» **Old-Age and Survivors Insurance (OASI) Trust Fund:** This fund consists of retirement and survivor payments.

» **Disability Insurance (DI) Trust Fund:** This fund is for disability insurance.

If the SSA collects more money than it needs for current payments, the surplus is invested in special U.S. Treasury bonds, which earn interest to help grow these funds.

What's the Difference between Social Security and Supplemental Security Income?

Social Security and Supplemental Security Income (SSI) are vital government programs for almost 75 million Americans. They serve different purposes and have different eligibility requirements.

Social Security is an earned benefit that people qualify for by working and paying Social Security taxes known as Federal Insurance Contributions Act (FICA). Social Security provides retirement, survivor, and disability benefits based on your (or your spouse's) work history and earnings. In general, the more you work and contribute, the higher your monthly benefit will be.

SSI is a needs-based program designed to assist older adults and people with disabilities who have limited income and resources. Different from Social Security, SSI does not require a work history; it's funded by general tax revenues. Monthly payments are usually lower. Many people who receive SSI also qualify for Medicaid.

Medicaid is run jointly by federal and state governments to provide health care and long-term care coverage for more than 78.5 million Americans, including children, parents, low-income adults, older adults, and people with disabilities. The government sets general standards for Medicaid, but specific eligibility requirements and coverage details vary by state. Your income must fall below certain levels to qualify. Each state has different rules for Medicaid eligibility, and in some cases even different names for the program, but it's usually based on your household income, age, disability, family size, and sometimes assets.

What Is the Social Security Fairness Act?

The Social Security Fairness Act was signed into law in January 2025. It's a major reform for restoring full Social Security benefits to millions of public servants such as teachers, firefighters, and police officers. These individuals were previously penalized under two provisions — the Windfall Elimination Provision (WEP) and the Government Pension Offset (GPO) — which previously reduced or eliminated benefits for people who worked in jobs not covered by Social Security.

Should I Be Worried about the Future of Social Security?

Many Americans are worried about the future of Social Security. According to the latest trustees report, ongoing income along with trust fund reserves will allow scheduled Social Security benefits to be paid until 2034.

Without Congressional action, Social Security would be able to pay about 81 percent of scheduled benefits in 2035 when the trust funds run out. Nobody wants such a sudden reduction in payments to more than 69 million Americans, so it's highly likely Congress will intervene.

Chapter **2**

Determining Whether You're Eligible

The first step to receiving Social Security benefits is determining whether you're eligible. This chapter answers questions regarding specific eligibility situations — including those who are still working, those who live outside the United States, those who are divorced, and more.

Can I Receive Social Security Benefits If I'm Still Working?

You can receive Social Security benefits while working, but how much you'll receive depends on your age and how much you earn. If you're under full retirement age (currently 67 for people born in or after 1960), your benefits may be reduced if you exceed the earnings limit. For 2026, the limit is $24,480 (for individual filers) and $1 is deducted for every $2 you earn above this limit.

This amount of the limit increases in the months prior to reaching your full retirement age. Your benefits are reduced by $1 for every $3 you earn above $65,160 in 2026. Note that these limits adjust with inflation yearly.

How Many Credits Do I Need to Qualify for Social Security?

As you work and pay taxes, you accumulate Social Security credits. You can earn up to four credits a year. After you've earned 40 credits after ten years of work, you qualify for retirement benefits. The years and the credits don't have to be consecutive. You can start working, stop for a while, and then return to work on and off and ultimately qualify.

In 2026, you get one credit for every $1,890 you earn in wages or self-employment income. The amounts are adjusted annually based on national wage trends.

Can I Receive Social Security Benefits If I'm Divorced?

If you were married at least ten years, you may be eligible to receive Social Security benefits based on your former spouse's earnings record. You also can file for these benefits starting at age 62, and your ex doesn't need to be notified. To qualify, your ex must be receiving their own Social Security benefits or be at least 62 years old, and you must have been divorced for at least two years. In addition, you must be unmarried.

An eligible former spouse can receive up to 50 percent of their former spouse's full retirement age benefit amount, regardless of whether the ex began collecting early. The payments you receive don't reduce the benefits of your ex or their current spouse, if they're remarried. However, if you're also eligible for benefits on your own work record, Social Security will pay the higher of the two amounts, not both.

Can I Receive Social Security Benefits If I'm a Noncitizen?

Noncitizens can receive Social Security benefits within the United States if they meet certain requirements. Generally, the individual must be lawfully present in the country and have earned at least 40 work credits (ten years of work) in jobs where Social Security taxes (FICA) were paid. The individual will also need a valid Social Security number and authorization to work in the United States.

If a noncitizen leaves the United States, they may still receive benefits, but there are restrictions. Benefits potentially can stop after six consecutive months abroad unless specific exceptions apply.

Can Multiple Spouses Claim Social Security Benefits Based on My Earnings History?

Multiple former spouses could claim Social Security on your work record if each marriage lasted at least ten years and the individuals meet the standard eligibility requirements.

It's important to note that benefits are separate from one another and a former spouse's claim doesn't reduce the amount another former spouse can receive, nor will it affect your own benefits or those of a current spouse. Each eligible ex may receive up to 50 percent of your full retirement age benefit amount, and Social Security handles each claim separately.

Can I Receive Social Security Benefits Based on My Spouse's Earnings?

You can receive Social Security benefits based on your spouse's earnings if they're already receiving retirement or disability benefits and you're at least 62 years old (or any age if you're caring for your spouse's qualifying child). The spousal benefit is up to 50 percent of your spouse's full retirement age benefit, but claiming before your own full retirement age will reduce the amount you'll receive. If you're eligible for both your own benefits and spousal benefits, Social Security will pay you the higher of the two, but not both.

Can I File for Spousal Payments under My Spouse's Account while I Delay My Own?

You can't file for spousal Social Security benefits while delaying your own. This is due to the *deemed filing rule,* which requires that you apply for your own retirement benefits and spousal benefits if you're eligible for both. You'll then receive the higher of the two amounts, but not both separately.

How Do I Qualify for Social Security Disability Insurance or Supplemental Security Income Benefits?

To qualify for benefits from either program, you must meet both medical and work history requirement, depending on if it's Social Security Disability Insurance (SSDI) or Supplemental Security Income (SSI). You can do this online, by phone, or in person. Here's a breakdown:

» **General medical requirements for both SSDI and SSI:** The condition must prevent you from engaging in substantial gainful activity. For 2026, this means earning more than $1,690 per month if you're not blind; the limit is $2,830 per month for individuals who are statutorily blind. If you're blind, you can get more information about eligibility at www.ssa.gov/people/blind.

The condition must be medically determinable and expected to last at least one year or result in death.

» **Work history requirements for SSDI:** SSDI eligibility depends on your work credits, which you earn by paying Social Security taxes. In 2025, you earn one credit for each $1,810 in wages or self-employment income, up to four credits per year. Most workers need 40 credits, with 20 earned in the last ten years before becoming disabled (the 20/40 rule). Younger workers may qualify with fewer credits:

- **Under age 24:** About six credits (one and a half years of work) in the three years before disability.

- **Ages 24 through 30:** You must have spent at least half the time since turning 21 in covered work.

- **Age 31 and older:** Generally, 20 credits in the last ten years.

Note: SSI does not require work credits. It's a needs-based program for people who are 65 or older, blind, or disabled, and who have limited income and resources. Resources must generally be worth no more than $2,000 for an individual or $3,000 for a couple, excluding your home and one vehicle. Income limits vary by state, but the federal SSI payment standard in 2026 is $994 per month for an individual and $1,491 for a couple.

Chapter **3**

Applying for Social Security

After you've determined that you're eligible for Social Security (see the preceding chapter), you're ready to apply. This chapter fills you in on all the information you need to complete the application process, no matter which type of benefit you're applying for.

What Documents Do I Need to Apply for Benefits with the Social Security Administration?

When you're applying for Social Security, the documents you need vary based on the benefit. Commonly required documents include the following:

» Proof of age (for example, a birth certificate)

» Social Security number (SSN; either your Social Security card or an official record such as a tax form or employment record)

» Proof of U.S. citizenship or lawful immigration status, such as a passport, birth certificate, certificate of citizenship, certificate of naturalization, consular report of birth abroad, or certification of birth abroad

» Bank account information (for direct deposit)

Additional documents are required depending on the type of Social Security benefit you're applying for (see the following sections).

How Do I Apply for Social Security Benefits?

Depending on the benefit you're applying for, you can apply for Social Security benefits online with a *my* Social Security account (www.ssa. gov/myaccount), by phone at 800-772-1213, or in person at your local Social Security Administration (SSA) field office (appointments are recommended).

To apply for Social Security retirement benefits, you'll need:

» W-2 forms or self-employment tax returns from the previous year

» Military service papers (if applicable)

» Marriage certificate (if you're applying for spousal benefits)

TIP

You can apply for retirement benefits as early as four months in advance, and you don't need to have all your documents ready at the time of application. Social Security can sometimes help you obtain them later.

How Do I Apply for Social Security Survivor Benefits?

Survivor benefits provide support to widows, widowers, children, and in some cases dependent parents of a deceased worker. You can apply for these benefits by phone at 800-772-1213 or in person at your local SSA field office; there is no online process to apply for these benefits as of 2026.

To apply for Social Security survivor benefits, you'll typically need the following:

» Proof of death (for example, a death certificate)
» SSNs (both yours and the deceased's)
» Birth certificate for yourself, the deceased, and any dependents
» Marriage certificate
» Bank info for direct deposit

You may also need the following:

» W-2s or tax returns of the deceased
» Birth or adoption records (for children)
» Proof of support (for dependent parents)
» Military discharge records

How Do I Apply for Social Security Benefits Online?

To apply online for Social Security, the easiest way is with a *my* Social Security account (www.ssa.gov/myaccount). First, you must create or log into your personal *my* Social Security account. After you're logged in, you'll be able to apply for retirement, Social Security Disability Insurance (SSDI), or spousal benefits. The online process guides you step-by-step and allows for saving your progress and returning later if necessary. You'll need the required documentation, too.

How Do I Apply for Social Security Benefits If I'm a Caregiver?

As a caregiver of someone else, such as an aging parent or an individual with a disability, you can help them apply for Social Security benefits. If they want you to act as their official representative with the SSA, you must file Form SSA-1696 (www.ssa.gov/forms/ssa-1696.pdf), which authorizes you to communicate with the SSA and manage the application or a claim on their behalf. If the application is approved and the person can't manage their own benefits, the SSA will appoint a representative payee to receive and manage the payments on their behalf.

You can assist them through the application process by helping them determine the type of benefit they qualify for, gathering the necessary documentation, and applying online with a *my* Social Security account (www.ssa.gov/myaccount).

How Do I Apply for Social Security Benefits If I'm a Veteran?

As a veteran applying for Social Security benefits, the same general rules for civilians still apply. You can apply online with a *my* Social

Security account (www.ssa.gov/myaccount), by phone at 800-772-1213, or in person at your nearest SSA field office.

How Do I Apply for Social Security Benefits If I'm a Student?

You can't apply for Social Security benefits based solely on your student status. There are other specific situations, however, in which students may be eligible using the common documentation and additional school enrollment verification (if applicable):

» **Survivor benefits:** If a parent or guardian by whom you were legally adopted has passed away, you could be eligible for benefits up to age 18.

» **Disabled adult child (DAC) benefits:** If you're age 18 or older, you're unmarried, and you have a disability that began before the age of 22, you may be eligible for benefits based on a parent's Social Security record.

» **Supplemental Security Income (SSI):** If you're a student with a qualifying disability with limited income or resources, you may be eligible for SSI.

How Do I Apply for Social Security Benefits If I'm a Parent?

Applying for Social Security benefits as a parent can vary depending on your situation:

» **If you're caring for a child under 16 or a child with a disability,** you could qualify for benefits based on your spouse's or even former spouse's record. You can do this online with a *my* Social Security account (www.ssa.gov/myaccount), by phone at 800-772-1213, or in person at your local SSA field office.

If you're applying for benefits for a child with a disability, you must complete a Child Disability Report and provide their medical and school records. For SSDI, the parent is retired, disabled, or deceased and the child's disability began before the age of 22. These reports can be done online or over the phone. After you submit the report, an SSA rep will contact you by phone to begin the application process. You can also call them to apply or schedule an appointment.

» **If you're the surviving parent of a deceased worker,** there are very limited circumstances under which you may be eligible for survivor benefits; you must apply by phone or in person.

How Do I Apply for Social Security Benefits If I'm a Stepparent?

As a stepparent, you may be eligible to apply for Social Security benefits on behalf of your step-child if the biological or adoptive parent (your spouse) is currently receiving Social Security retirement or disability benefits or has passed away. The child would need to meet the student requirements and have lived with or received half of their support from you before benefits began or the parent passed away.

To apply, you'll need the following:

» The child's birth certificate and SSN
» Your marriage certificate
» Proof of the child's support and dependency

How Do I Apply for Social Security Benefits If I'm a Grandparent?

As a grandparent raising a grandchild, you can apply on their behalf if the child's parents are deceased or disabled or you've legally adopted the child. The child must be living with you before turning 18 and you must have provided at least half of the child's financial support for the year before the month you became entitled to Social Security retirement or disability benefits.

If the child is under 1 year old, you must have been providing at least half of their support since birth. If the parents are living, the child's parents must not be making regular contributions for the child's support.

To apply, you'll need the following:

» Your SSN and proof of identity
» The child's birth certificate and SSN
» Proof of your relationship to the child (for example, adoption papers)
» Documentation showing that the child's parents are deceased or disabled (if applicable)
» Financial records showing that you provided at least half of the child's support

How Do I Apply for Social Security Benefits If I'm a Legal Guardian?

As a legal guardian applying for Social Security benefits for a child, you must apply to become a representative payee. This is the case even if you have legal guardianship already, because legal guardianship alone does not authorize you to manage benefits. You can apply to become a representative payee by submitting the SSA-11 form (www.ssa.gov/payee/faqrep.htm). You'll also need to provide documentation like your ID, proof of guardianship, the child's birth certificate, and medical/legal documents (if applicable).

After you're approved as the representative payee, you can apply for benefits on their behalf (such as disability or SSI) online with a *my* Social Security account (www.ssa.gov/myaccount), by phone at 800-772-1213, or in person at your local SSA field office. Disability and SSI claims can start online, but they may require follow-up by phone or at your local SSA office. Survivor benefits must be applied for by phone or in person.

In certain cases, if the child's parents are deceased, have disabilities, or are not providing support, and you've been providing at least half of the child's care, you may qualify to apply for benefits on the child's behalf.

How Do I Apply for Social Security Benefits If I'm a Foster Parent?

As a foster parent planning to apply for Social Security benefits on behalf of a child in your care, how you apply will depend on the type of benefit and your legal relationship to the child. In most cases, foster parents aren't automatically eligible to apply for a child unless they're appointed as a representative payee by the SSA.

However, there are SSI benefits for children in foster care who are disabled or blind. You'll need documentation showing the child's foster care status and expected end date. To qualify for SSI benefits the child must

» Live in foster care

» Have a qualifying disability or blindness

» Be within 180 days of losing foster care eligibility

» Appear likely to meet all nonmedical SSI requirements after foster care payments stop

How Do I Check the Status of My Social Security Application?

To check your application status, log in to your *my* Social Security account at www.ssa.gov/myaccount. You'll see updates like your filing date, current claim location, and any scheduled hearings. If you don't have an account, you can create one for free. You can also call Social Security directly at 800-772-1213 if you prefer to speak with a representative.

How Do I Apply for Medicare through Social Security?

You can apply for Medicare online at www.ssa.gov/medicare, even if you're not ready to start retirement benefits. The process takes around 10 to 30 minutes and usually doesn't require documentation. Your Initial Enrollment Period is seven months total — it starts three months before the month of your 65th birthday and ends three months after.

How Long Does It Take to Receive Social Security Benefits after Applying?

Processing times can vary. The SSA aims to process retirement applications within two to four weeks, but many people report waiting four to five months or longer, especially during high-volume periods or if additional verification is needed. You can check your status online at www.ssa.gov/myaccount, call 800-772-1213, or visit your local SSA field office for updates.

Decoding Social Security Benefits

2

IN THIS PART . . .

If you're like most people, when you think of Social Security, you think of retirement benefits — and with good reason: Retirement benefits are a huge part of what Social Security offers. But Social Security provides disability benefits and survivor benefits, too. This part walks you through all the benefits offered by Social Security, one by one.

Chapter **4**

Retirement Benefits

etirement benefits are what most people think of when they think of Social Security. This chapter explains what the retirement benefit is, at what age you're eligible, what happens if you delay retirement benefits, and more.

What Is the Social Security Retirement Benefit?

Social Security retirement benefits are monthly payments most Americans receive later in life, typically after they've left the workforce. To qualify, you need to have worked and paid Social Security taxes — most often Federal Insurance Contributions Act (FICA) or Self-Employed Contributions Act (SECA) — for at least ten years (earning 40 credits). The amount you receive depends on how much you've earned over your lifetime and the age at which you start collecting benefits.

What Is the Retirement Age for Social Security?

You can start collecting Social Security retirement benefits as early as age 62, but your monthly payments will be reduced for life if you do. To get your full benefit amount, you'll need to wait until your full retirement age (see the next section).

What Is the Social Security Full Retirement Age?

Your full retirement age is the age at which you can start receiving 100 percent of the Social Security retirement benefit calculated from your lifetime earnings history, without any reduction. It depends on your birth year:

If you were born . . .	Your full retirement age is . . .
Between 1943 and 1954	66 years
1955	66 years and 2 months
1956	66 years and 4 months
1957	66 years and 6 months
1958	66 years and 8 months
1959	66 years and 10 months
1960 or later	67 years

TIP

Claiming benefits at your full retirement age ensures that you'll receive 100 percent of the amount you're entitled to based on your lifetime earnings.

What Is the Social Security Retirement Age for Maximum Benefits?

To receive the highest possible monthly payment, you should wait until at least age 70 to start collecting Social Security retirement benefits. By delaying past your full retirement age, you earn delayed retirement credits that increase your benefit by 8 percent per year. After age 70, there's no further increase, so 70 is considered the optimal age for maximizing your monthly payments if you can afford to wait.

What Is the Social Security Retirement Age for Reduced Benefits?

You can start receiving Social Security retirement as early as age 62, but your monthly payments will be permanently reduced. This reduction depends on how many months before your full retirement age you begin collecting. For example, if your full retirement age is 67 and you start collecting at 62, your benefits could be reduced by up to 30 percent, *permanently.*

What Is the Social Security Retirement Age for Earning Delayed Credits?

Delayed retirement credits refer to the increase in your monthly Social Security payments when you wait after your full retirement age to claim. Each month you delay past your full retirement age, your future benefit increases, up to a total of 8 percent per year. These credits grow your benefit amount until age 70.

TIP

This strategy can significantly boost your lifetime income, especially if you expect to live into your 80s or beyond.

What Are the Benefits of Delaying Social Security Retirement Benefits?

Delaying Social Security retirement benefits beyond full retirement age (see "What Is the Social Security Full Retirement Age?," earlier in this chapter) increases your monthly benefit through delayed retirement credits. Benefits increase by 8 percent annually until age 70. This can result in a significantly higher lifetime payment, especially for those who live longer. Delaying also boosts survivor benefits for your spouse and may offer better financial security in later retirement years.

What Is the Social Security Retirement Age for Spousal Benefits?

Spouses can begin receiving Social Security benefits based on a partner's work record as early as age 62. However, just like regular retirement benefits, claiming early results in a reduced amount. The most you can get is 50 percent of your spouse's full retirement benefit, and to receive that, you must wait until *their* full retirement age.

What Is the Social Security Retirement Age for Divorced Spouse Benefits?

If you're divorced, you were married for at least ten years, and you haven't remarried, you may be eligible for benefits based on your former spouse's work record, starting at age 62. The rules are similar to those for spousal benefits, and the amount you receive will depend on the age at which you claim.

TIP

You don't need your former spouse's permission, the Social Security Administration (SSA) will not notify them that you've claimed, and claiming doesn't affect their benefits.

What Is the Social Security Retirement Age for Widow/ Widower Benefits?

Surviving spouses can begin receiving Social Security survivor benefits as early as age 60 (or age 50 with a qualifying disability). Full survivor benefits are available at your full retirement age. You also can choose to switch between survivor benefits and your own retirement benefits later, depending on which provides a higher monthly payment. You can't receive both survivor benefits and your own Social Security benefit at the same time in full.

Chapter **5**

Disability Benefits

As of April 2025, 7.2 million disabled workers received Social Security benefits. That's 10.3 percent of people collecting Social Security. So, although it's not a huge piece of the pie, it's still a significant number, and it's a benefit you should take advantage of if you're eligible. This chapter explains what the benefit is, how the Social Security Administration (SSA) determines eligibility, and how far back benefits extend.

What Is Social Security Disability Insurance?

Social Security Disability Insurance (SSDI) is a federal program administered by the SSA that provides monthly payments to individuals who are unable to work due to a qualifying long-term disability. To be eligible, you must have a medical condition expected to last at least a year or result in death and you must have earned enough work credits through prior employment where you paid Federal Insurance Contributions Act (FICA) taxes.

What Are Social Security Disability Insurance Benefits?

SSDI benefits are based on an individual's past earnings. Dependents such as spouses and children may also qualify for auxiliary benefits. Applications can be submitted online with a *my* Social Security account (www.ssa.gov/myaccount), by phone at 800-772-1213, or in person at your local SSA field office.

TIP

Many initial claims are denied, but an appeals process is available.

What Is the Social Security Disability Determination Process?

The Social Security disability determination process begins when an individual submits a claim. Social Security verifies nonmedical eligibility, such as age and work history. If those requirements are met, the claim is then sent to a state Disability Determination Services (DDS) office, where medical evidence is obtained from doctors about the disability. DDS also arranges consultative exams. If the claim is approved, SSA calculates and begins benefits; if the claim is denied, the claimant has the option to appeal through a process called *reconsideration.*

What Is the Social Security Disability Evaluation Review Process?

The review process assesses whether a claimant continues to meet the disability criteria. The SSA uses a five-step sequential evaluation, examining the severity of the medical condition, ability to perform past work, and capacity to adjust to other work. This includes evaluating *residual functional capacity,* which measures what the claimant can still do despite limitations. SSA considers physical, mental, and environmental factors, along with age, education, and work experience, in determining residual functional capacity.

What Is the Social Security Disability Vocational Review Process?

Vocational review is part of the SSA's five-step evaluation, specifically steps 4 and 5. The SSA assesses whether the claimant can perform past relevant work or adjust to other work based on age, education, and residual functional capacity. If vocational evidence is insufficient, the SSA may develop additional work history or proceed to Step 5, using medical-vocational guidelines to determine disability status.

What Is the Social Security Disability Work Review Process?

The SSA reviews work activity to determine if a beneficiary is engaging in substantial gainful activity, which may affect eligibility. During a nine-month trial work period, any month with earnings over $1,210 in 2026 counts, but benefits continue. After the trial period, earnings above the substantial gainful activity level ($1,690 per month in 2026 or $2,830 if blind) may lead to suspension or termination of benefits. The SSA also considers work incentives and re-entitlement periods to support beneficiaries attempting to return to work.

What Is the Social Security Disability Continuing Disability Review Process?

The SSA conducts Continuing Disability Reviews (CDRs) periodically to determine if a beneficiary still meets the medical criteria for disability.

Reviews typically occur every three years or every five to seven years if improvement is not expected. The SSA uses Form SSA-454 or SSA-455 to gather updated medical and financial information. If SSA finds the individual is no longer disabled, benefits may stop.

If I Receive a Retroactive Disability Determination, How Far Back Will Social Security Pay Benefits?

If you receive a retroactive disability determination, the SSA may pay benefits back 12 months before the application, depending on when the disability began and when you applied. This doesn't vary by medical condition, but it does depend on proving that the disability existed during that time. For SSDI, there's a mandatory five-month waiting period from the established onset date before the benefits begin. Supplemental Security Income (SSI) does not allow retroactive payments.

Chapter **6**

Survivor Benefits

Social Security survivor benefits can be a big help to spouses and children after someone dies. The Social Security Administration (SSA) paid survivor benefits to 5.8 million people as of April 2025. This chapter explains what the survivor benefit is and how it works.

What Is the Social Security Survivor Benefit?

Social Security survivor benefits provide monthly payments to eligible family members of a deceased worker who paid into the Social Security system. These benefits are available to spouses, divorced spouses, children, and dependent parents. The amount received depends on the deceased person's earnings record and the age and relationship of the survivor. In addition to monthly payments, survivors may also qualify for Medicare based on the deceased person's work history. A one-time lump-sum death payment of $255 may also be available to a surviving spouse or child.

How Does Social Security Handle Benefits for Children of Deceased Parents or Guardians?

Children may qualify for survivor benefits if a parent who worked and paid Social Security taxes dies. Eligible children include those under age 18, those ages 18 to 19 who are full-time students in high school, and those of any age who became disabled before age 22. Benefits are generally paid until the child turns 18 or graduates from high school, whichever comes later. Under certain conditions, stepchildren, adopted children, grandchildren, and step-grandchildren may also qualify. The average monthly benefit for a child is around $1,100, and applications must be made by phone at 800-772-1213 or in person at your local SSA field office.

If My Spouse Dies Before I Do, Will I Be Eligible to Collect Survivor Payments?

You may be eligible for survivor benefits if your spouse dies and they worked and paid Social Security taxes. As a surviving spouse, you can begin receiving benefits as early as age 60 (or age 50 if you have a disability), and at any age if you're caring for the deceased person's child who is under 16 or disabled. The benefit amount ranges from 71.5 percent to 100 percent of your spouse's benefit, depending on when you start collecting. You may also qualify for Medicare and a one-time death payment of $255.

3

Making Sense of Your Payments

IN THIS PART . . .

This part is all about Social Security payments, including how they're calculated and the taxes you'll have to pay on your Social Security benefits. It also covers some special circumstances like what happens if you get divorced while receiving spousal payments for Social Security or what happens if you retire outside the United States. Finally, it walks you through what to do if Social Security denies your disability claim.

Chapter **7**

How Benefits Are Calculated

When you're applying for Social Security benefits, knowing how much you'll receive can feel like a mystery. But there's nothing mysterious about it. The Social Security Administration (SSA) uses specific formulas to determine your benefit — this chapter spells it out. It also clarifies the cost-of-living adjustment, the earnings limit, and more.

How Are Social Security Benefits Calculated?

Social Security retirement benefits are based on your lifetime earnings. The SSA looks at your highest 35 years of earnings, adjusts them for wage growth, and calculates your average indexed monthly earnings (AIME). That number is then used in a formula to determine your primary insurance amount (PIA); this is the base amount you'll receive at full retirement age. The more you earn and the longer you work, the higher your benefit will be.

What Is the Maximum Social Security Benefit?

The maximum monthly Social Security benefit depends on the age you start collecting. In 2026, the maximum benefit is $4,152 if you retire at full retirement age, $3,082 if you start at age 62, and $5,521 if you wait until age 70. To qualify for the maximum, you must have earned the maximum taxable income in FICA taxes for at least 35 years, which is the wage cap set each year. For the year 2026, that amount is $184,500. Note that this amount changes each year.

What Is the Social Security Cost-of-Living Adjustment?

The cost-of-living adjustment (COLA) is an annual increase in Social Security benefits to help keep up with inflation. It's based on changes in the Consumer Price Index for Urban Wage Earners and Clerical Workers (CPI-W). For 2026, the COLA is 2.8 percent, which means most beneficiaries saw a modest increase in their monthly payments starting in January.

What Is the Social Security Earnings Limit?

If you're under full retirement age and still working while receiving Social Security, there's a limit to how much you can earn before your benefits are reduced. In 2025, the limit is $23,400. If you earn more than that, the SSA deducts $1 for every $2 over the limit. If you reach full retirement age during the year, the limit increases to $62,160, and the deduction is $1 for every $3 over that amount.

What Is the Social Security Family Maximum?

The family maximum is the total amount that can be paid to a family based on one worker's earnings record. If multiple family members (like a spouse and children) qualify for benefits, the SSA may reduce each person's payment to stay within the maximum. This limit ensures that total payments don't exceed a set percentage of the worker's benefit.

What Is the Social Security Earnings Test?

The earnings test applies if you're receiving Social Security and working before reaching full retirement age. It determines how much of your benefit may be withheld based on your income. The withheld benefits aren't lost; they're added back into your monthly payments after you reach full retirement age. This test helps balance early benefit claims with continued work.

How Does the Social Security Administration Calculate Disability Benefits under Social Security Disability Insurance?

The SSA calculates your monthly retirement benefit using a formula based on your AIME from your 35 highest-earning years. These earnings are adjusted for inflation, and then the AIME is applied to a progressive formula with three "bend points." For someone first eligible for retirement or disability benefits in 2026 (or who dies in 2026 before becoming eligible), the primary insurance amount (PIA), which is the monthly benefit you'd receive at full retirement age, is calculated as 90 percent of the first $1,286 of AIME, plus 32 percent of AIME between $1,286 and $7,749, plus 15 percent of AIME above $7,749.

Claiming earlier or later than your full retirement age adjusts this amount down or up.

What Is the Social Security Delayed Retirement Credit?

Delayed retirement credits increase your monthly Social Security benefit if you wait to claim after your full retirement age. For those born in 1943 or later, the benefit increases by 8 percent per year until the age of 70.

TIP

Waiting to collect Social Security until age 70 can significantly boost your lifetime income, especially if you live into your 80s or beyond.

What's the Maximum Social Security I Can Receive?

In 2026, the maximum Social Security retirement payment you can receive depends on your earnings history and the age at which you start claiming benefits. If you earned the maximum taxable income for at least 35 years and you wait until age 70 to claim, you could receive up to $5,181 per month. Claiming at your full retirement age of 67, you would yield a maximum of $4,207 per month, but claiming age 62 would reduce your benefit maximum to $2,969 per month.

What If I Worked at a Job That Didn't Pay into Social Security during My Career?

If you worked a job that didn't pay into Social Security, such as certain government positions, nonprofit or religious organizations, or employment abroad, you may not qualify for Social Security benefits unless you also had enough work in jobs that did pay into the system. To be eligible for retirement benefits, you generally need at least 40 work credits, which equals about ten years of covered employment.

Previously, if you had a pension from a non-covered employer, your Social Security benefits could be reduced under the Windfall Elimination Provision (WEP) or the Government Pension Offset (GPO). However, this changed with the Social Security Fairness Act, signed into law in January 2025, which eliminated both WEP and GPO. As a result, pensions from non-covered jobs no longer reduce your Social Security benefits starting in 2024. If you qualify for benefits based on other covered work, you'll now receive the full amount without offsets. Many affected beneficiaries received retroactive payments and higher monthly benefits in 2025.

Chapter **8**

Taxes and Withholding on Benefits

Social Security isn't free — you'll have to pay tax on your earnings. Uncle Sam giveth, and Uncle Sam taketh. This chapter explains everything to do with Social Security and taxes.

Can I Have My Taxes Deducted from My Social Security Payments?

You can request to have federal income taxes withheld voluntarily from your Social Security payments. You can do this by submitting the Internal Revenue Service (IRS) Form W-4V (www.irs.gov/pub/irs-pdf/fw4v.pdf) to your local Social Security Administration (SSA) field office. You can elect to have 7 percent, 10 percent, 12 percent, or 22 percent of your monthly payment withheld voluntarily.

Do Taxes on My Social Security Depend on the State I Live In?

Determining whether your Social Security payments are taxed at the state level depends on the state you live in. Federal taxes on Social Security payments are based on your income level, but up to 85 percent of your benefits may be taxable if your combined income exceeds certain thresholds. In 2026, eight states still tax Social Security benefits: Colorado, Connecticut, Minnesota, Montana, New Mexico, Rhode Island, Utah, and Vermont.

How Does Self-Employment Income Affect Social Security Taxes and Benefits?

When you're self-employed, you're viewed as both the employer and employee, so you'll have to pay both sides of Social Security and Medicare taxes, which equals 15.3 percent of net earnings. If you make $400 or more in a year, you're responsible for reporting it in order to earn the Social Security credits you need to qualify for benefits.

How Do I Report Self-Employment Income to Social Security?

If you're self-employed, report your earnings when you file your federal tax return. Use Schedule SE to calculate your Social Security and Medicare taxes. You must report net earnings of $400 or more to earn credits toward future benefits. These earnings help determine your eligibility and benefit amount.

Does Receiving Social Security Benefits Affect the Taxation of Other Retirement Income?

Receiving a Social Security check doesn't affect your pension or retirement account withdrawals — those are taxed separately. But your total amount of income can then influence whether your Social Security benefits themselves are taxable. The IRS uses a formula based on your combined income to determine how much of your benefits are subject to tax. Pensions and retirement withdrawals, again, are taxed separately.

How Is the Taxable Amount of Social Security Benefits Determined?

The IRS uses combined income to determine how much of your benefits are taxable. This consists of your adjusted gross income (AGI), any tax-free interest, plus half of your Social Security benefits. If your total hits more than $25,000 for single filers or $32,000 for married couples, you may owe taxes on up to 50 percent of your benefits. Go past $34,000 (or $44,000 for married couples), and up to 85 percent could be taxable. But here's the silver lining: No matter how much you make, you'll never be taxed on more than 85 percent of your Social Security benefits.

Chapter **9**

Special Circumstances and Exceptions

Some people's Social Security situation is straightforward, but if yours doesn't fit the usual pattern, this chapter is for you. It covers how the Social Security Administration (SSA) handles less typical circumstances, including same-sex marriages and domestic partnerships, divorce after benefits begin, retiring abroad, combining Social Security with unemployment, and special credits for military service. If you fall into any of these categories, this chapter will set your mind at ease.

How Does a Same-Sex Marriage or Domestic Partnership Affect Social Security Spousal or Survivor Benefits?

Same-sex marriages are fully recognized by the SSA. Individuals in a legally valid same-sex marriage are eligible for the same spousal and survivor benefits as opposite-sex couples.

What Happens If I Get Divorced while Already Receiving Spousal Payments for Social Security?

If you're receiving Social Security spousal payments and you get divorced, your eligibility may continue if the marriage lasted for at least ten years. You may also be eligible to receive benefits on your former spouse's record if you don't remarry after the divorce and meet requirements such as being 62 or older. However, if you remarry, those benefits typically stop unless the new marriage ends or you qualify under special survivor rules.

You can find more information about understanding your unique eligibility questions at www.aarp.org/social-security.

TIP

What Happens to My Social Security Benefits If I Retire Abroad?

Generally, if you retire abroad, you'll continue to receive your Social Security benefits. (There are a few restricted nations where payment is not allowed. You can check eligibility at `www.ssa.gov/foreign`.)

If you're not a U.S. citizen, your ability to receive benefits abroad depends on your country of citizenship and whether the country has a Social Security agreement with the United States. Additionally, you must report changes in address, marital status, or work activity to the SSA, and you may be required to periodically verify your status through mailed questionnaires.

What Are the Consequences of Receiving Social Security Benefits while Also Receiving Unemployment Benefits?

You can generally receive both Social Security and unemployment benefits, because they both serve a different purpose. Social Security provides retirement or disability income, while unemployment supports those actively seeking work after job loss. However, some states may reduce unemployment payments if you're receiving Social Security retirement benefits or Social Security Disability Income (SSDI).

How Are Social Security Credits Handled for Military Veterans Who Served during Wartime and Received Special Extra Earnings Credits?

These special extra credits for military veterans who served during wartime were for the period 1940 to 2001 and for those in active duty. The SSA automatically applied these credits for veterans who served after 1956 and had active duty with pay.

Chapter **10**

Filing Appeals

This chapter explains the appeals process step-by-step for a number of scenarios. You may choose to work with an attorney or other qualified person to help you with the appeal.

How Do I Appeal a Social Security Decision?

If you disagree with a decision, you can request an appeal online or by submitting Form SSA-561 (Request for Reconsideration; www.ssa.gov/forms/ssa-561-u2.pdf). Appeals must be filed within 60 days of receiving the decision letter.

There are four levels of appeal, outlined in the following section. The appeals process can take months or even years. Visit www.ssa.gov/appeals for details.

What Is the Social Security Disability Appeal Process?

If your disability claim is denied, you have four levels of appeal:

1. Reconsideration
2. A hearing before an administrative law judge (ALJ)
3. Review by the Appeals Council
4. Filing a civil suit in federal court

Each level allows you to present new evidence and arguments. The process begins with a request for reconsideration and continues sequentially if you disagree with each decision.

What Is the Social Security Disability Reconsideration Process?

Reconsideration is the first step in appealing a denied claim. It involves a complete review of the original claim and any new evidence by a different Disability Determination Services (DDS) team than the one that made the initial decision. You must make your request for reconsideration within 60 days of receipt of the denial notice. You can do so online at www.ssa.gov/forms/ssa-561.html. Or, if you prefer, you can download Form SSA-561 (Request for Reconsideration) at www.ssa.gov/forms/ssa-561-u2.pdf, print it, and mail it to the SSA or file it in person at your local SSA field office.

What Is the Social Security Disability Hearing Process?

If the reconsideration is denied, you can request a hearing before an ALJ. This hearing allows you to present any evidence, testify, and bring witnesses, including medical or vocational experts. Hearings currently can be conducted in person, by phone, or by video. The ALJ reviews all evidence and issues a decision. You must request a hearing within 60 days of the reconsideration decision. You do that by filing Form HA-501 (Request for Hearing by Administrative Law Judge), which you can download at www.ssa.gov/forms/ha-501.pdf.

TIP

You can find more information at www.ssa.gov/forms/ha-501.html or by calling or visiting your local field office.

What Is the Social Security Disability Appeals Council Process?

If the ALJ denies your claim, the next step is to request a review by the Appeals Council within 60 days. You do that by filing Form HA-520 (Request for Review of Hearing Decision/Order), which you can download at www.ssa.gov/forms/ha-520.pdf. The Appeals Council may deny the request if it finds the ALJ's decision was correct, or it may review the case and issue a new decision or send it back to the ALJ for further review. The Appeals Council considers all issues from the hearing, including those decided in your favor.

TIP

You can find more information at www.ssa.gov/forms/ha-520.html.

What Is the Social Security Disability Federal Court Review Process?

If the Appeals Council denies to review or upholds the ALJ's decision, you can file a civil suit in your U.S. district court. This is the final level of appeal. You must file the suit within the judicial district where you reside or have a principal place of business (or in Washington, D.C., if no district applies). The SSA prepares the case record for court, and you must send certified copies of the complaint and summons to the SSA's Office of General Counsel.

Although it isn't required, you have the right to professional representation in your dealings with the SSA. This could be an attorney or a disability advocate who isn't a lawyer but has passed an SSA-administered exam and met other educational and occupational requirements.

4

Managing Your Social Security

Odds are, you'll have to get in touch with the Social Security Administration at some point — whether you need to request a new Social Security card, you're a victim of identity theft, or you move or change your name or experience any of the myriad other changes that come with being alive. This part has you covered.

Chapter **11**

Working with the Social Security Administration

etting in touch with the Social Security Administration (SSA) is a routine part of managing your benefits, but knowing the right way to do it can save time and frustration. Whether you need a new Social Security card, want to check your Social Security statement, or suspect fraud, this chapter explains the fastest, safest ways to reach the SSA.

How Do I Contact the Social Security Administration?

You can reach the SSA in several ways. The easiest is through their website at www.ssa.gov, where you can apply for benefits, check your application status, request documents, and manage your account. If you prefer to speak with someone, call the national toll-free number at 800-772-1213 (TTY: 1-800-325-0778), Monday through Friday, 8 a.m. to 7 p.m. local time. You can also visit your local SSA field office, but appointments are recommended unless your idea of fun is waiting in line.

Does Social Security Still Send Paper Statements?

Social Security still mails paper statements, but only to certain individuals. Those individuals are age 60 or older, not receiving benefits, and don't have a *my* Social Security account (www.ssa.gov/myaccount). If you aren't receiving benefits and don't have a *my* Social Security account, the SSA will automatically mail you a paper statement about three months before your 60th birthday.

How Can I Review My Social Security Statement?

To view your Social Security Statement online, create or log in to your *my* Social Security account at www.ssa.gov/myaccount. The statement shows your earnings history and estimated future benefits.

What Are Reasons to Go into the Field Office versus Doing Things Online?

You can do a lot online, including applying for benefits, updating direct deposit, and requesting a replacement card. But there are still important reasons to visit a field office in person. Some reasons to go in person include verifying your identity, dealing with a complex situation (such as applying for benefits on behalf of someone else), or dealing with issues such as benefit fraud appeals or disability claims that require documentation or personal assistance.

How Do I Get a New Social Security Card?

If you're applying for the first time from inside the United States, you can apply online and go to a local SSA field office to provide your documentation. After your application is approved, you'll receive a Social Security card with your number on it by mail within 14 days.

If you're a U.S. citizen age 18 or over with a mailing address and no name change, the most convenient way to receive a replacement Social Security card is to apply through your *my* Social Security account. If you can't apply online, you can complete Form SS-5 and submit it by mail or in person at your local SSA field office. You can request a replacement Social Security card up to three times per year and ten times in your lifetime.

How Do I Replace a Lost or Stolen Social Security Card?

If your Social Security card is lost or stolen, you can make a request for a replacement online, by mail, or in person. The most secure and fastest method is through your *my* Social Security account (www.ssa.gov/myaccount). This option is available to U.S. citizens age 18 or older with a U.S. mailing address and no name change. If you can't complete this request online, you can fill out Form SS-5 and submit it by mail or in person at your local SSA field office with proof of identity.

How Do I Protect My Social Security Number from Identity Theft?

To protect your Social Security number (SSN) from identity theft, try keeping it in a safe place. Usually, just knowing your SSN is enough for verification. Only share your SSN when it's legally required and always ask why it's needed, how it will be used, and what will happen if you refuse to provide it.

If you suspect your SSN has been part of identity theft, you can ask SSA to block electronic access to your record by calling 800-772-1213. You can also consider putting a freeze on your credit report with the three major credit bureaus (Equifax, Experian, and TransUnion), monitoring your financial accounts regularly, and using strong passwords that have multifactor authentication.

What Should I Do If I Suspect Someone Is Fraudulently Using My Social Security Number?

If you suspect someone is fraudulently using your SSN, you should immediately review your Social Security statement at www.ssa.gov/myaccount. Report anything unfamiliar to the

SSA. You should also file a report with the Federal Trade Commission (FTC) online at https://identitytheft.gov to create a recovery plan. Contact the Internal Revenue Service (IRS) at 800-908-4490 if you also suspect tax fraud. If misuse of your SSN is found, report it to the SSA's Office of the Inspector General at https://oig.ssa.gov or by calling 800-269-0271.

If you get a text, email, or call purportedly from the SSA about misuse of your SSN, it's almost certainly a scam.

How Do I Report Fraud to the Social Security Administration?

You can report fraud, waste, or abuse to the Office of the Inspector General by calling 800-269-0271 (TTY: 1-866-501-2101), submitting a report online at https://oig.ssa.gov, or mailing details to the Social Security Fraud Hotline, P.O. Box 17785, Baltimore, MD 21235-7785. Reports can be made anonymously.

DID YOU KNOW?

It's best to report changes with the Social Security Administration by the tenth day of the month after it occurs to avoid any issues with your benefits.

Chapter **12**

Reporting Changes to the Social Security Administration

Change happens, and when it does, the Social Security Administration (SSA) usually wants to hear about it. Whether you've moved, changed your name, switched banks, gotten married or divorced, or had a shift in income, keeping the SSA up to date helps ensure your benefits are accurate and keep coming on time. This chapter walks you through these changes and how to keep the SSA in the loop.

How Do I Change My Name with the Social Security Administration?

To change your name with the SSA, you'll have to complete a few steps in person or by mail — you can't do it online. First, you'll need to fill out Form SS-5 (Application for a Social Security Card), which is available for download at www.ssa.gov/forms/ss-5.pdf. Then submit the form along with original documents proving the legal name change (for example, a marriage certificate, a divorce decree, or a court order) and identification such as a U.S. driver's license or passport to your local SSA field office.

How Do I Change My Address with the Social Security Administration?

The fastest method for changing your address with the SSA is through your *my* Social Security account (www.ssa.gov/myaccount). You can update your contact information in the My Profile section. You can also call SSA toll-free at 800-772-1213 or visit your local SSA field office.

How Do I Correct My Date of Birth with the Social Security Administration?

To correct your date of birth with the SSA, you'll need to request a replacement Social Security card so your record can be updated. In addition to the application, you'll need to submit documents that prove your age (birth certificate, passport, and identity).

You can begin the process by calling the SSA at 800-772-1213 to speak with a representative or by making an appointment at your local SSA field office. Most cards arrive within 14 days after the SSA approves the application.

How Do I Change My Direct Deposit Information with the Social Security Administration?

You can change your direct deposit information for Social Security benefits through two secure options, both of which are designed to protect against fraud and ensure timely payments. The most efficient option is to log into your *my* Social Security account (www.ssa.gov/myaccount) and update your banking information under the Direct Deposit section. Alternatively, you can visit your local SSA field office.

How Do I Report Changes in My Income to the Social Security Administration?

If you receive Supplemental Security Income (SSI), and you've had an income change, you must report that change to the SSA in order to avoid incorrect payments or penalties. You must report monthly wages by the tenth day of the following month through your *my* Social Security account (www.ssa.gov/myaccount), through the SSA Mobile Wage Reporting app, by calling the automated phone line (866-772-0953), or by calling 800-772-121.

If you're an SSDI beneficiary, you should report any work or income changes promptly by phone or with Form SSA-795 online or at a local field office.

If you're a retirement beneficiary under full retirement age, you must notify SSA if your earnings exceed the annual limit of $24,480 in 2026 (or $65,160 in the year you reach full retirement age) through your online account or by phone.

If your income drops due to a life-changing event like retirement, file Form SSA-44 to request a lower Medicare premium.

TIP

Report these changes as quickly as possible to avoid overpayments or benefit disruptions.

How Do I Report a Change in Marital Status to the Social Security Administration?

To report a change in marital status to the SSA, you'll need to contact the SSA directly by calling 800-772-1213, visiting your local SSA field office, or mailing a written notice with your Social Security number (SSN) and supporting documentation (marriage certificate or divorce decree) to your local office.

TIP

It's important to submit this information as quickly as possible. Not reporting the change promptly may result in incorrect payments or penalties.

How Do I Report a Change in Household Composition to the Social Security Administration?

Usually for SSI, when reporting a change in household composition (someone moving in or out of your home) to the SSA, you should so by the tenth day of the month after the change to ensure benefits are accurate and timely. You can do this by calling SSA at 800-772-1213, visiting your local SSA field office, or mailing a written notice with your SSN and relevant documentation to your local office.

You can find the mailing address for your local office by entering your zip code in the SSA's online office locator at `https://secure.ssa.gov/ICON/main.jsp`.

How Do I Report a Change in Employment Status to the Social Security Administration?

Reporting a change in employment status to the SSA is usually required for individuals receiving SSI or Social Security Disability Insurance (SSDI), because that work activity can affect eligibility and payment amounts. Similar to changes in household composition, you should notify the SSA as soon as possible. You can do this by calling the SSA at 800-772-1213, visiting your local SSA field office, or mailing a written notice with your SSN and relevant documentation to your local field office.

How Do I Report a Change in Health Status to the Social Security Administration?

A change in health status is relevant to individuals receiving SSI or SSDI benefits. To report a change in health status, such as entering or leaving a hospital, nursing home, or other medical facility, notify the SSA as soon as possible to avoid eligibility or incorrect payment amounts — ideally by the tenth day of the month after the change occurs. You can do this by calling 800-772-1213, visiting your local SSA field office, or uploading documentation through your *my* Social Security account (www.ssa.gov/myaccount).

How Do I Report a Change in Financial Status to the Social Security Administration?

If you receive SSI, you must report any changes in your financial status to the SSA. This includes changes in income, account balances, bank accounts, and ownership of stocks, bonds, or certificates of deposit (CDs). These changes can affect your eligibility and payment amount. You can report financial changes through your *my* Social Security account (www.ssa.gov/myaccount), by calling 800-772-1213, or by visiting your local SSA field office with supporting documents — ideally by the tenth day of the month after the change occurs.

How Do I Report a Change in Citizenship Status to the Social Security Administration?

To report a change in citizenship or immigration status to the SSA, you'll usually need to request a replacement Social Security card so your record can be updated. You can start this process by calling the SSA at 800-772-1213 and informing the representative that you want to update your citizenship or immigration status.

How Do I Report a Change in Dependent Status to the Social Security Administration?

To report a change in dependent status (such as a child no longer being eligible for benefits, a change in custody, or a dependent with Social Security turning 18), send the SSA a short statement explaining the nature of the dependent change and when it happened. You can report this by calling the SSA at 800-772-1213 or visiting your local SSA field office. In most cases, the SSA rep will fill out Form SSA-795 and ask you to sign it. You can also download and complete the form yourself. Supporting documents (such as custody papers, marriage or divorce certificates, or school attendance verification for a child over 18) could be required. You can upload documents online through your *my* Social Security account or handle it in person.

How Do I Report a Change in Benefit Eligibility to the Social Security Administration?

To report a change in benefit eligibility, such as becoming newly eligible for a benefit or no longer qualifying for benefits, you should contact the SSA directly. This is important for individuals receiving survivor benefits, disability benefits, or SSI. You can report the changes by calling SSA at 800-772-1213 or by visiting your local SSA field office.

How Do I Report the Death of a Social Security Beneficiary?

To report a death, call the SSA at 800-772-1213 or contact your local SSA field office. Funeral homes often report deaths using Form SSA-721 (Statement of Death by Funeral Director), but family members can also notify the SSA directly. Reporting promptly helps stop payments and may initiate survivor benefits for eligible family members.

Index

Connecticut, taxation, 58

Consumer Price Index for Urban Wage Earners and Clerical Workers (CPI-W)., 53

contact details updation, 74

Continuing Disability Reviews (CDRs), 42–43

cost-of-living adjustment (COLA), 53

credits

delayed retirement credits, 36

for qualify, 12–13, 16

D

date of birth correction, 81

death report updation, 87

deceased parents with children, survivor benefits, 46

deceased worker, parent of, 25

delayed retirement credits, 36, 55

delaying benefits, 37

dependent status update, 86–87

direct deposit information changes, 81

disability

benefits calculation, 54–55

claim, 65

Disability Determination Services (DDS), 40–41, 66

Disability Insurance (DI) Trust Fund, 6

disabled adult child (DAC) benefits, 24

divorced spouses

benefits updating, 38

divorce after benefits begin, 62

retirement benefits, 38

Social Security benefits, 13

documents, Social Security benefits, 20

domestic partnerships, 62

M

marital status changes, 83

maximum benefits, 52

  retirement, 35

maximum retirement payment, 55–56

Medicaid, 7–8

Medicare

  apply for, 30

  survivor benefits, 46

military veterans, 64

Minnesota, taxation, 58

Montana, taxation, 58

N

name change, Social Security benefits, 80

New Mexico, taxation, 58

noncitizens, 13–14

O

online appeal submission, 65–66

online application, Social Security benefits, 22

P

parent application process, 25

police officers, benefits for, 8

primary insurance amount (PIA), 52, 55

processing times, 30

public servants, benefits for, 8

R

reconsideration, 41, 66–67

reduced benefits, retirement, 36

residual functional capacity, 41

retirement age, 34

retirement benefits. *See* Social Security retirement benefits

retiring abroad, 63

retroactive payments, 43

reviews work activity, 42

Rhode Island, taxation, 58

U

unemployment benefits, 63–64

U.S. citizenship proofs, 20

U.S. Department of the Treasury, 6

Utah, taxation, 58

V

Vermont, taxation, 58

veteran application process, 23–24

vocational review, 41–42

W

widow/widower, survivor benefits, 38

Windfall Elimination Provision (WEP), 8, 56

working people, Social Security benefits, 12

Publisher's Acknowledgments

Senior Managing Editor:
Kristie Pyles

Executive Editor:
Tracy Boggier

Editor: Elizabeth Kuball

AARP Contributor:
Jammie Lyell

Production Editor:
Tamilmani Varadharaj

Cover Design and Image:
Wiley

Special Help:
Carmen Krikorian